Return of the Liberators
1945 - 2015

A photographic record of veterans returning to the Netherlands

on the 70th Anniversary of Victory in Europe

Design and Photography by Keith Collman

The London Taxi Benevolent Association For War Disabled

Charity Commission No. 264678

Return of the Liberators 1945 - 2015

Design and photography by Keith Collman

www.keithcollman.com

First Published in the United Kingdom 2016 by Keith Collman Publishing
8 King's Avenue, Hemel Hempstead, Hertfordshire, HP3 9TN, England

kc@keithcollman.com

600 copies in this First Edition

For Private Circulation

ISBN: 978-0-9563667-1-9

Design, layout and photography: Keith Collman

Repro, print and binding: PWP FS Print and Design, Hoddesdon, EN11 0BZ, England

Cover image: Scottish Piper Chic Mackie, 1st Bn. Black Watch, leading the Taxis on their return home.

Acknowledgements

The veterans and their families.

To the people who have sponsored and helped in the planning and organisation of the trip, they are as follows.

Netherlands

National Liberation Museum, Groesbeek
Sporthotel Papendal
Municipalities of Arnhem, Renkum, Wageningen and Groesbeek
Airborne Museum Hartenstein, Oosterbeek
Museum en Military Home Bronbeek, Arnhem
Hans Wiggers
Frans Ammerlaan
Robin Ammerlaan
Roger Beets
Karel Riksen
Gerrit Eijmers
Reymond Verhoef
Monique van Zoest
Ray Waller, Royal British Legion, Holland Branche
Henk van de Beek (4 - 5 mei wagn.)
Cees Aalbers en OSV Onder Ons
Brigitte van Veggel
Police Gelderland Midden, Arnhem
National Police, Driebergen
Airborne Commemoration Foundation, Oosterbeek
Police Sports Association 'Renkum' Oosterbeek
Market Garden Foundation, Arnhem
Orange Committee Heteren
Orange Committee Oosterbeek
Airborne Battle Wheels Oosterbeek
Van Amerongen Facilities, Arnhem
BritNed Ltd. Arnhem
Gelderland TV
Koninklijke Harmonie Oosterbeek
Lt. General Ted Meines (ret.)
Burgemeester Herman Kaiser
Driebergen Rijk Middelman
Dolphin Barber Mates

UK

The National Lottery
The Big Lottery Fund
The Royal British Legion
Commonwealth War Graves Commission
Millwall Football Club
Union Jack Club
Royal Hospital Chelsea
Parkeston Railway Club, Harwich
The Colchester Band
The Blackfriar
Jennie Flory
Liz Hawkins
Keith Collman
Rachel Jones
Face Communications (2007) Ltd. of Stevenage
Susy Goodwin

Sponsors

(Contributed over £500 for the trip or £1,000 in total)

Audrey Sherry, Camberfeld Taxis (Chris Hearnden), Stena Line, Morrisons Supermarket (Harwich), Parkeston Railway Club, North Cheam Sports and Social Club (Tony Millard), Peter Howes (Bill Parr), A & S Services (Hoddesdon), Millwall F.C., Matt and Pauline Bickerton, P J Hayman (Insurance), Dave Allen, LTDA Licenced Taxi Drivers Association, Taxi Insurance Companies who waved the Green Card fee for most of the taxis.

Foreword

As a Patron of the London Taxi Benevolent Association for the War Disabled, it is my great pleasure to provide a few words of introduction to this marvellous photographic record of a quite unique journey. I was privileged to travel in 2015 with the taxi drivers and veterans on the final Return of the Liberators trip to mark the 70th anniversary of the liberation of the Netherlands in 1945.

The spectacle of 90 black cabs and 120 veterans crossing the channel and processing from the Hook van Holland to Arnhem was quite amazing and Keith Collman has captured the images of the trip in the most wonderful way. Sincere thanks go to him and, of course, to the organisers, and the many cabbies and collectors who not only gave their time and effort to make this trip so successful but also continue to sustain the charity on a day-to-day basis.

Finally, the whole trip was focused on recognising and honouring those veterans who helped liberate the Netherlands in the final months of the war. Many made the ultimate sacrifice and never came back but some of those who did made the journey again in 2015. This wonderful book records that journey and I commend it without reservation.

Vice-Admiral Sir Adrian Johns KCB CBE DL - Patron

Charity History

The London Taxi Benevolent Association for War Disabled was formed in 1948 at the Bedford Arms Pub, Fulham by London Licensed Taxi drivers.

Their object then, as now, was to help war disabled both at home and in hospitals throughout London and the Home counties by providing friendship and support wherever possible. Our aim is simple, to work for the benefit, comfort and enjoyment of the war disabled and veterans to the best of our ability and to assist with the help of grants and specialist equipment where possible.

We hold an annual outing to Worthing in June where over 300 ex-service men and women from all over London - including the Royal Hospital Chelsea - are taken to the town in a fleet of 130 London cabs, for lunch and a day of entertainment and friendship.

Our Guests of Honour in previous years have included HRH Prince Philip, HRH Princess Alexandra, HRH Duchess of Kent, Sir Douglas Bader, Group Captain Sir Leonard Cheshire and many other celebrities from the world of sport, theatre and television.

We have also organised trips to former battlegrounds in France and the Netherlands when veterans from all over the UK and Ireland were invited to join us.

We are proud to acknowledge that the aims started back in 1948 are still alive today and will continue while members of the London taxi trade are willing and able to give their time and commitment to help those who have given so much for their country.

The Charity Committee

Honorary Chairman: Gary Belsey
Assistant Chairman: Dave Hemstead
Honorary Life President: Harry Joel MBE
Honorary Secretary: Paul Davis
Assistant Secretary and Press Officer: Derek Leone
Honorary Treasurer: Michael Husk

Vice Presidents

Dick Goodwin
Reg Hay
Eddie Hillery

Committee Members

Gary Hutchins
Dennis James
Graham Pike
Terry Ward, Transport Officer
Dennis Hayes
Aaron Capell
Ian Parsons

The Return of the Liberators 1945 - 2015

Concept for the Trip

After a very successful five day trip to France in May 2008 to commemorate the VE-Day celebrations in Normandy I considered the concept to see if this success could be achieved again in a different part of the European Theatre of operations during World War Two, The Netherlands.

Having travelled for many years to Arnhem, to commemorate the anniversary of the battle there each September, I had built up a number of contacts in the area. I asked Frans Ammerlaan of the Market Garden Foundation if he thought a trip would be possible, he agreed, saying the veterans would be very warmly received by the Dutch people as they were eternally grateful to our World War Two veterans, along with veterans from Canada, Poland and America, for their liberty in 1945.

In August 2010 I took the idea of a trip to The Netherlands to the committee and proposed that we aim for it to take place to run in conjunction with the Dutch Liberation services and celebrations to be held on the 4th and 5th May. As 2011 would have been a too shorter period to arrange the trip and gather the finances together we set our sights for May 2012 and gave this project the name of 'Veterans Return – The Netherlands 2012'

As we needed to arrange the finances for the trip we knew that we would have to get out to the stations, both mainline and underground, and the football grounds to start collecting. We managed to assemble a fantastic group of veteran collectors who turned out time and time again, some of them from 7am, in all weathers to collect for us.

Therefore in May 2012, with our finances secure and with the aid of grants from the Royal British Legion and Heroes Return we were able to take 144 World War Two veterans in 92 taxis for a five day trip to celebrate Dutch Liberation.

The depth of the welcome we received from the Dutch was immeasurable, they took the veterans to their hearts and many friendships and bonds were made. We were asked to return in 2013 but this was impossible as we didn't have the time to organise a trip of this magnitude nor have the finances available to be able to afford it.

As our band of collectors continued to turnout for us on a regular basis we were able to run another trip for all service veterans, including our World War Two group, in May 2014.

Since we were taking younger veterans along with us, 90 WW2 and 58 other veterans accompanied us, we were able to play a much bigger role in the Liberation Parade at Wageningen on the 5th May which was much applauded by the crowds.

Could we manage this one more time, it would be a great shame to miss an anniversary year such as the 70th in 2015. The decision was taken, not lightly, to run the trip one more time and start the planning process. We knew our numbers of veterans would have to be lower to enable us to take the carers that some of our group would now need to accompany them for the trip.

We were also aware that this would definitely be the last time this could happen on this scale as the Dutch National Police, who had escorted us on the two previous occasions could no longer offer us their help after 2015.

Our finances were now secure with the help of a grant from The Royal British Legion and the Heroes Return fund.

We would never have the opportunity to gather these wonderful men and women together again and offer them the chance to return to the Netherlands for possibly the last time. With all the obstacles now considered we had to go all out for this final trip.

The 'Return of the Liberators 1945 – 2015' was underway.

Having known Keith's work for many years, we approached him about the possibility of creating a book to celebrate the trip. It is due to his attention to detail, sympathy with his subject and wonderful photography that we now have this remarkable record of a unique gathering of World War Two veterans.

Dick Goodwin - Vice President

The Collectors

The three trips to The Netherlands would never have been possible without the fabulous work and support of our collectors who turned out for us time after time to collect funds from Joe Public for our charity.

Where they have passed on, their year of death is indicated.

Harry Arnold	Harry Bailey	Sid Belsey
Syd Blackmore (2014)	Buzz Brown (2016)	Jack Bruce (2014)
I/P Roy Cadman	I/P Sam Cameron	Harry Card
Brian Carter	Charlie Carter	Mick Clarke
James Corrigan	Tom Cromie (2015)	Ernie Davis
John Dibble	Les Eastwood	Brian Fletcher
Dickie Forrester	John Gillett	Peter Gospel
Harry Grew	Wally Harris MM (2014)	Eddie Hillery (now Vice President)
Joe Hoadley	I/P John Honey	Charlie Jefferies
Peter Kent	Roy Knight	Arthur Letchford
Bill Martin (2016)	Bert Mayle	Don McAdie (2014)
Danny McCrudden	Eddie Mortimer	Vic Needham-Crofton
John O'Connor	Bill Parr	Allan Parsons
George Parsons	Sylvia Parsons	Jeff Pattinson
Frank Pendergast	Alan Reid	Ted Roberts (2015)
Ron Robinson	Tom Schaffer	George Seal (2015)
Harry Silvester (2014)	Bert Smith	George Stagg
Norman Topliss (2014)	I/P Fred Walker (2015)	Ken Watts
I/P Reg Wilderspin	I/P Bill Woods	Colin Wright
Jenette Wright	John Wynne	Len Wynne

I/P - In Pensioner, Royal Hospital Chelsea

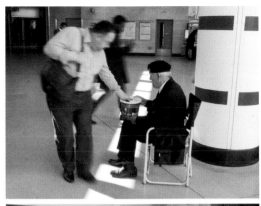

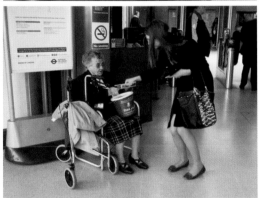

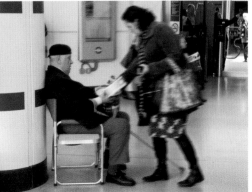

The Drivers

Our charity came into being and exists for the sole benefit of our wonderful veterans, many of whom saw service in World War Two. We take these men and women on trips, outings and lunches offering friendship and support where ever and whenever possible.

The deepest gratitude and appreciation must however, go to the Licenced London Taxi drivers, without whom our charity would cease to function. The loyalty and support provided by these fantastic men and women is exceptional and we doubt if it could be surpassed by any other group of volunteers.

They give their time and their vehicles freely and cheerfully and are only compensated for fuel, even this many refuse to accept. The relationship between veteran and driver often continues long after the scheduled outings are over. Firm and lasting friendships are formed with drivers continuing the spirit of the charity in their own time.

In this we have unassailable proof that London Licenced Taxi drivers are the finest in the world and we salute them.

James Anam	Gerry Dunn	Chris Hearnden	Terry Millington	Paul Ray
Michael Bailey	Paul Dupuis	Brian Heffernan	James Moore	Keith Riches
David Barr	Robert Fitzgerald	Michael Hemstead	Anthony Neal	John Saunders
Daniel Bedford	Brian Flanagan	John Hill	Anthony Offredi	Derek Seymour
Greg Boud	Ken Flemwell	Peter Holley	Stephen O'Hagan	Frederick Short
David Bowker	Scott Flemwell	Trevor Hooley	Carlos Oliveira	Michael Small
Aaron Capell	Paul Gale	John Hurley	Roberto Oliveira	Richard Stark
Peter Carey	Ian Gillam	George Iddiols	Silvi Oliveira	Reade Stephenson
Richard Chamberlain	Patrick Granger	Karl James	Les Orr	Keith Tickner
David Clegg	Ian Gray	Fred Jones	Alan Osborne	Stephen Turvell
Jason Cook	Derek Gunn	Martin Jones	Ian Parsons	Norman Waghorn
Frank Costella	Steve Hanson	Paul Kenealy	Barbara Paterson	Peter Waterfield
Raymond Coster	Glyn Harris	Stewart Lewis	Joe Pengelly	Bernie Watterson
Derrick Dane	John Harris	Julian Lillington	James Pullum	David Webb
Bob Deeney	Anthony Havis	Bernard McKay	Jackie Quaile	Douglas Wright
John Dixon	Peter Havis	Gary Mankelow	Janet Ramsden	David Tullett (mech)
Stephen Dolby	Simon Hawes	Kevin Miller	James Rainbird	

The Veterans

ALLEN Peter
Service: Army - 14459801
Regt: Royal Signals, 6th Arm. Div.
Rank: Cpl.
DoB: 23.6.1927

Anslow John
Service: Army - 14684822
Regt: 90th Field Regt. R.A.
Rank: Gunner/Tank Driver
DoB: 7.7.1922

ASHLEIGH Frank
Service: Army - 14417002
Regt: 'A' Sqn. Glider Pilot Regt., Army Air Corps
Rank: Sgt.
DoB: 23.12.1924

BAILEY Charles
Service: Army - S/14713635
Regt: R.A.S.C., 58 BSD
Rank: N.C.O.
DoB: 23.1.1926

BAILEY Harry
Service: Army - T264941
Regt: R.A.S.C. Pioneer Corps Coy.
Rank: Driver
DoB: 18.6.1921

BAREFIELD Frederick Henry (Fred)
Service: Army - 19079444
Regt: 11th Para. Sqn. Royal Engineers
Rank: Sapper
DoB: 15.7.1927

BARTON George
Service: Army - 4750967
Regt: 7th Bn. K.O.S.B. 1st Airlanding Bde. 1st A.B. Div.
Rank: Sgt.
DoB: 13.10.1919

BEALL Walter (Wally)
Service: Royal Navy - DMX 580236
Regt: Tank Landing Craft LCT 836
Rank: Leading Wireman/Gunner
DoB: 21.2.1924

BENFORD Charles
Service: Army - 6019174
Regt: 2nd Bn. Essex Regt.
49th West Riding 'Polar Bears'
Rank: Sgt.
DoB: 12.7.1919

BONNER Iain
Service: Army - 14423232
Regt: 'D' Sqn. Glider Pilot Regt., Army Air Corps
Rank: Sgt.
DoB: 13.7.1923

BRACE Leonard (Len)
Service: Army - 14540130
Regt: Royal Signals. II Air Form'n Signal Regt.
Rank: Driver
DoB: 13.8.1924

BROOKER Dennis
Service: Army - T/14456447
Regt: R.A.S.C. 16th Parachute Bde.
Rank: Sgt.
DoB: 18.11.1925

BROWN Edwin
Service: Army - 14457139
Regt: 1st Bn. Parachute Regt.
Rank: Pte.
DoB: 1.12.1925

BROWN Henry (Buzz)
Service: Royal Navy - DMX577654
Regt: Comb Opps. 330 Support Sqn.
Rank: Wireman
DoB: 12.5.1925

BROWN Michael
Service: Army - 7948850
Regt: 'E' Sqn. Glider Pilot Regt., Army Air Corps
Rank: Sgt.
DoB: 5.11.1923

BRYANT Norman
Service: Royal Navy - PJX 383923
Regt: H.M.S. Collingwood, Victory 1 Siskin, Sparrowhawk, Tern, Heron, Daedelus
Rank: Able Seaman
DoB: 12.7.1924

CADMAN Stuart (Roy)
Service: Army - 6292857
Regt: The Buffs, No 3 Army Commando
Rank: Sgt. C.S.M.
DoB: 26.3.1923

CANTWELL William (Bill)
Service: Army - 14406039
Regt: 24th Field Regt. R.A.
Rank: L/Cpl.
DoB: 21.9.1923

CHITTENDEN James
Service: Army - 6031704
Regt: 1st Indep. Para. Platoon Pathfinder
Rank: Cpl.
DoB: 31.12.1923

COODE John
Service: Army - 14423128
Regt: 1st Bn. K.O.S.B.
Rank: Staff Sgt.
DoB: 16.5.1925

CORRIGAN James
Service: Army - 4470270
Regt: Durham Light Infantry
Rank: Pte.
DoB: 17.1.1924

COTTLE Geoffrey
Service: Army - 14429254
Regt: R.E.M.E.
Rank: Driver I.C.
DoB: 5.6.1925

COURT Alfred
Service: Army - 7947981
Regt: 3rd. Royal Tank, 15 Armoured Bde.
Rank: Cpl.
DoB: 1.2.1922

CROSSON John
Service: Army - 14648290
Regt: 7th Bn. K.O.S.B. 1st Airlanding Bde. 1st A.B. Div.
Rank: Pte.
DoB: 20.7.1924

CUTHBERT John
Service: Army - 6481591
Regt: Royal Fusiliers, Royal Signals R.E.M.E.
Rank: Sgt.
DoB: 27.9.1922

DAINES Reginald (Stan)
Service: Army - 14696417
Regt: 2nd Bn. Essex Regt., 4th Bn. Dorsets
Rank: Pte.
DoB: 9.9.1925

DANE Roland
Service: Army - 14426390
Regt: 7th Bn. Black Watch, 51st Highland Div.
Rank: Pte.
DoB: 23.7.1925

DAVIES Ernest (Ernie)
Service: Royal Navy - P/JC 430059
Regt: H.M.S. Cotton
Rank: Able Seaman
DoB: 18.3.1925

DIMARCO Luis
Service: Army - 14206503
Regt: 1st Bn. Parachute Regt., 1st A.B. Div.
Rank: Sgt.
DoB: 6.1.1923

EASTWOOD Les
Service: Royal Navy - D/MX 514454
Regt: H.M.S. Copra, Landing Craft
Rank: Leading Wireman
DoB: 7.12.1924

EMPSON George
Service: Army - 2044194
Regt: R.E.M.E. Att. 2/7th Bn. Middlesex Regt.
Rank: Sgt.
DoB: 8.11.1920

EVERSON Bertram (Bert)
Service: Army - 14392618
Regt: Royal Tank Regt.
Rank: Trooper
DoB: 12.8.1924

FAULKNER Frederick (Fred)
Service: Royal Navy - P/JX 274822
Regt: H.M.S. Argonaut & Whelp
Rank: Able Seaman Torpedoman
DoB: 26.11.1921

FORRESTER Richard (Dickie)
Service: Army - 6857976
Regt: 4th Armoured Bde. 2nd Bn. K.R.R.C.
Rank: Rifleman
DoB: 1.2.1926

FRANCIS Charlie
Service: Army - 14428604
Regt: R.A.S.C., 743 Coy.
Rank: Driver
DoB: 4.11.1926

FRENCH George
Service: Army - 14425564
Regt: King's Royal Rifle Corps
Rank: Cpl.
DoB: 9.9.1925

GARDNER Albert (Bert) (oldest Veteran on the trip)
Service: Army - 1879007
Regt: R.E. & R.W.A.F.F.
Rank: W.O. (C.M.S.)
DoB: 27.4.1918

GLADDEN Bill
Service: Army - 14337754
Regt: 6th Airborne Div., Armoured RECCE
Rank: Trooper
DoB: 13.1.1924

GLOVER Frederick (Fred)
Service: Army - 6300039
Regt: 9th Bn. Parachute Regt., 6th A.B. Div.
Rank: Sgt.
DoB: 23.12.1925

GRANGE John
Service: Royal Navy - C/JX 571571
Army: - 21182388
Regt: Comm. of Signals, Signal Staff,
Royal Signals 16 Ind. Para. Bde.
Rank: N/Signalman, A/Sgt
DoB: 1.2.1926

GREW Harry
Service: Royal Navy - C/KX 121086
Regt: H.M.S. Starwort/Westcott/Highway/Dido
Rank: Stoker Petty Officer
DoB: 26.2.1922

HACKER Donald (Don)
Service: Army - 14386258
Regt: Ox. & Bucks. L.I., 6th A.B. Div.
Rank: Pte.
DoB: 21.12.1923

HARPER Henry
Service: Army - T/14643742
Regt: R.A.S.C., A.B. 1st Div. & 6th Div.
Rank: Driver
DoB: 13.4.1924

HARRIS Frederick (Fred)
Service: Army - 14232650
Regt: 621 Field Sqn., 7th Arm. Div., R.E.
Rank: Driver/W.O. Sgt.
DoB: 28.8.1922

HART Walter
Service: Army - 7266147
Regt: R.A.M.C.
Rank: L/Cpl.
DoB: 12.8.1918

HARTLEY Alan
Service: R.A.F. - 3011060
Regt: 271 Sqn. Transport Command
Rank: L.A.C.
DoB: 17.8.1924

HAWARD Jeffrey M.M.
Service: Army - 6204205
Regt: Middlesex Regt. 51st HighLand Div.
Rank: Sgt.
DoB: 28.7.1919

HAWKINS Frederick (Fred)
Service: Army - 14511135
Regt: Royal Engineers
Rank: Cpl.
DoB: 6.1.1924

HERBERT Harold
Service: Army - 14296059
Regt: 10th Bn. Para. 4th Bde., 1st A.B. Div.
Rank: Pte.
DoB: 30.3.1924

HIGGINS Pat
Service: Army - 14454607
Regt: R.A.M.C.
Rank: Sgt.
DoB: 26.9.1926

HOSGOOD Dennis
Service: Army - 14499323
Regt: Queen's Own Cameron Highlanders
Rank: Pte.
DoB: 15.5.1926

HUTCHINSON Arnold (Arnie)
Service: Army - 147012259
Regt: 7th Bn. (L.I.) Para. Regt., 6th A.B. Div.
Rank: Pte.
DoB: 17.9.1924

JACKSON Wilfred (Wilf)
Service: Army - 14386125
Regt: R.A.M.C. 146 Field Amb. 49 Infy.
Rank: Sgt.
DoB: 22.7.1924

JEFFRIES Charles (Charlie)
Service: Army - 6923151
Regt: Highland Light Infantry, 53rd Welsh Div.
Rank: Sgt.
DoB: 8.3.1922

JEFFRIES John
Service: Army - 2379610
Regt: Royal Corps of Sigs., 4th Para. Bde., 'K' Section
Rank: Signalman
DoB: 22.3.1922

JOHNSON Ronald
Service: Army - M 623468
Regt: 'E' Sqn. Glider Pilot Regt., Army Air Corps
Rank: Lt. then Captain
DoB: 9.10.1921

KENDALL John (Jack)
Service: Army - 14422452
Regt: 179th Field, R.A.
Rank: Bombardier
DoB: 10.2.1926

KENNEDY David
Service: Royal Navy - DJX 564503
Regt: H.M.S. Domett, Arctic Convoys
Rank: Able Seaman
DoB: 19.3.1926

KENNEDY Ernest (Ernie)
Service: Royal Navy - D/JX 559406
Regt: DEMS Naval Gunner Defence Eq Merchant Ships
Rank: Able Seaman
DoB: 12.7.1925

KENT Peter
Service: Royal Navy - DJX 564384
Regt: H.M.S. Adventure & Hartland Point
Rank: Able Seaman
DoB: 20.4.1925

The Veterans

KERSH Mervyn
Service: Army - 14628122
Regt: 17 Transit Veh. Prk. 17 Adv. Ord. Depot R.A.O.C.
Rank: Sgt. A/WO
DoB: 20.12.1924

KNOX James (Jim)
Service: Army - 6298287
Regt: Royal East Kent 'Buffs', 4th Bn. Para. Regt.
Rank: Pte.
DoB: 21.11.1924

KUBINSKI Henry
Service: Army - 22293656
Regt: 65 Coy, R.A.S.C., 18 Amphib Coy.
612 Tank Trans Coy. R.C.T. 16 Tank Trans Sqn. R.C.T.
Rank: S/Sgt.
DoB: 22.11.1925

LAMBETH Alex
Service: Merchant Navy - R254028
Regt: Troop Ships, Att. O.H.M.S.
Rank: Seamans Book
DoB: 3.12.1923

LEE Alfie (Fred)
Service: Royal Navy - CKX 613567
Regt: H.M.S. Nith, River Class Frig. Landing Craft H.Q.
Rank: Leading Stoker
DoB: 30.7.1926

LEWIS Percy
Service: Army - 5392782
Regt: 1st Bucks. Bn., 1st Bn. Black Watch
Rank: Signaller
DoB: 22.12.1922

LINES George
Service: Army - 2601640
Regt: Royal Signals, H.Q. 4th Army Group R.A.
Rank: Lance Corporal
DoB: 28.9.1923

LONSDALE Alfred (Alf)
Service: Royal Navy - P/JX 515589
Regt: H.M.S. Valiant. Malaya, Tyne Berwick & Glengyle
Rank: L/Seaman
DoB: 12.5.1925

McALLISTER Joseph
Service: Army - 14302764
Regt: 3rd Bn. Para. Regt., A Coy., 1 Plat., 1st A.B. Div.
Rank: Pte.
DoB: 7.2.1924

McCRUDDEN Danny
Service: Royal Navy - DJX 423232
Regt: H.M.S. Queensborough & Implacable
Rank: Able Seaman
DoB: 28.6.1924

MALIN Abba Myer
Service: Army - 14260367
Regt: 49th West Riding Div. 52nd Div., R.A.
Rank: Bdr.
DoB: 30.9.1923

MARSHALL Ernie
Service: Army - 1790266
Regt: 52nd Beds Yeomanry Heavy Regt. R.A.
Rank: Gunner
DoB: 30.8.1920

MARTIN Lawrence
Service: Army - 4547501
Regt: Div. Signals, 1st A.B., Div. Sigs.
Rank: Pte.
DoB: 22.10.1923

MARTIN William (Bill)
Service: Army - 14641592
Regt: 7th Bn. (L.I.) Para. Regt., 6th A.B. Div.
Rank: Pte.
DoB: 29.5.1924

MILLER Douglas Roy
Service: Royal Navy - PJX 298234
Regt: P'Mouth Div., R.N., H.M.S. Ganges,
Collingwood, Indomitable, Bramble
Rank: Able Seaman (Gunnery Div.)
DoB: 15.12.1923

MORGAN Ernest (Ernie)
Service: Army - S/14729499
Regt: R.A.S.C.
Rank: Pte., Cpl. on Demob.
DoB: 2.10.1925

MOSS Percy
Service: Army - 1452253
Regt: 55th Anti-Tank Regt., The Polar Bears
Rank: Gunner
DoB: 26.2.1920

PAGE Desmond (Des)
Service: Army - 7955918
Regt: 'E' Sqn. Glider Pilot Regt., Army Air Corps
Rank: Staff Sgt.
DoB: 7.7.1923

PARSONS George (Rev.) (husband to Sylvia below)
Service: Army - 6460965
Regt: No 2 Army Commando, Royal Fusiliers
Rank: Cpl.
DoB: 10.8.1919

PARSONS Sylvia (wife to George above)
Service: R.A.F. - LAC 450005
Regt: R.A.F.
Rank: L.A.C.
DoB: 25.7.1921

PATTINSON Geoffrey (Geoff)
Service: Army - 14503782
Regt: 9th Bn. Para. Regt., 6th A.B. Div.
Rank: Sgt.
DoB: 15.4.1924

PENDERGAST Frank
Service: Army - 14437981
Regt: 7th Bn. (L.I.) Para. Regt., 6th A.B. Div.
Rank: Pte.
DoB: 31.8.1925

PHIPPS Thomas (Tom)
Service: Army - 14489202
Regt: The Queen's Royal Regt.
Rank: Pte. Driver
DoB: 14.1.1927

PIERI Edward (Ted)
Service: Army - T/14442901
Regt: 250 Comp 1st A.B. Div. 63 Comp 6th A.B. Div.
Rank: Pte.
DoB: 8.5.1926

PRICE Walter
Service: R.A.F. - 18944442
Regt: 294 Sqn. Air Sea Rescue
Rank: L.A.C.
DoB: 17.12.1924

PULZER Geoffrey
Service: Army - 7948779
Regt: 23rd Hussars, 29th Armoured Bde.
Rank: Corporal
DoB: 6.7.1923

PYNE Harold
Service: R.A.F. - 611995
Regt: 43 Sqn. B of B H.M.S. Argus - Malta Convoys
Rank: Cpl.
DoB: 9.1.1921

READY Patrick
Service: Royal Marines - CH/X113577
Regt: Royal Marine Commando N458 Flotilla LCP
Rank: Marine
DoB: 24.2.1925

REID Alan
Service: Royal Navy - C/KX 639164
Regt: H.M.S. Balsam K72 Flower Class Corvette
Rank: Able Seaman
DoB: 18.2.1925

RICE Harry
Service: Army - 5774931
Regt: 4th Norfolks R.A., 1st Bn. Para. Regt., 1st A.B. Div.
Rank: Pte.
DoB: 31.3.1922

RILEY John
Service: Army - 14591335
Regt: Anti-Tank Regt. R.A.
Rank: Gunner D/O
DoB: 19.2.1925

ROBERTS Geoffrey
Service: Army - 14434693
Regt: 7th Bn. K.O.S.B., 1st Airlanding Bde., 1st A.B. Div.
Rank: Pte.
DoB: 28.7.1925

ROGERS Father Edward (Ted)
Service: Merchant Navy
Rank: 3rd Officer (3rd Mate)
DoB: 9.11.1924

SCHAFFER Thomas (Tom)
Service: Army - 14754673
Regt: Parachute Regt.
Rank: Pte.
DoB: 25.4.1926

SEALEY Joe
Service: Army - 14669481
Regt: Royal Signals, 129 Infantry Brigade, Signals
43rd Wessex Infantry Div.
Rank: Dvr/OP
DoB: 3.8.1925

SLEEP John
Service: Army - 2149206
Regt: Parachute Regt. Att. 1st Bn. Norfolk Regt.
Rank: Cpl.
DoB: 26.1.1921

SMITH Rosalind (Lyn)
Service: R.A.F. - 2161889
Regt: 12th Sqn.
Rank: ACW1
DoB: 25.11.1926

SMOOTHY Peter
Service: Royal Navy - C/MX 107794
Regt: HMLST 215 (Landing Ship Tank)
Rank: Leading Writer
DoB: 19.11.1924

SPRING William (Bill)
Service: Army - 1116198
Regt: 323 Bty. 81st Field Regt. R.A., 53rd Welsh Div.
Rank: L/Bdr Gunner/Driver/Mech
DoB: 1.11.1921

STAGG George
Service: Army - 14242082
Regt: 168 Coy. Royal Engineers
Rank: L/Cpl.
DoB: 1.12.1923

STANNARD William (Bill)
Service: Army - 14879580
Regt: 1st Bn. Royal Fusiliers
Rank: Fusilier
DoB: 5.6.1926

STASZKIEWICZ Konstanty
Service: Army - 28521/30/l Attenstation 1369
Regt: 3rd Bn. Paratroop Bde. (1st Polish Indep.)
Rank: Cpl.
DoB: 30.10.1924

STEVENS Reginald
Service: Army - 1100580
Regt: 120th L.A.A. Regt. R.A.
Rank: Gunner Full Sgt.
DoB: 8.4.1921

STEVENS Robert (Bob)
Service: Army - 6107690
Regt: Royal Engineers
Rank: Driver/Operator
DoB: 26.9.1922

THIRKETTLE Len B.E.M.
Service: Army - 14831055
Regt: R.A.M.C.
Rank: Pte.
DoB: 13.8.1926

TOOKE Douglas
Service: Army - 5960781
Regt: 6th A.B. Div., RECCE Regt.
Rank: Cpl.
DoB: 16.8.1923

TURRELL Donald (Don)
Service: Army - 14217563
Regt: Cameronians, Scottish Rifles, 46th H'Land
Inf. Bde.,15th Scottish Inf. Div.
Rank: Cpl.
DoB: 27.7.1925

UNDERWOOD Leslie (Les)
Service: Royal Navy - JX 662507
Regt: D.E.M.S
Rank: Gunner
DoB: 2.3.1926

WALKER Fred
Service: Army - 5960542
Regt: Beds & Herts, No 3 Army Commando
Rank: Pte.
DoB: 29.7.1924

WASHER Kenneth (Ken)
Service: Army - 14379214
Regt: 1st A.B. Div., RECCE Sqn.
Rank: Trooper
DoB: 27.4.1923

WATTS Kenneth (Ken)
Service: Army - 14646425
Regt: 2nd Bn. Devonshire Regt.
Rank: L/Cpl.
DoB: 2.3.1925

WEEDEN Laurence (Laurie)
Service: Army - 2080390
Regt: 'F' Sqn. Glider Pliot Regt., Army Air Corps
Rank: Sgt.
DoB: 6.6.1922

WELLS James
Service: Royal Navy - MX 534923
Regt: H.M.S. Ambitious & Cleopatra
Rank: Leading Hand
DoB: 15.10.1924

WEST Kenneth
Service: Army - 14638023
Regt: 11th Bn. Royal Scots Fusiliers
Rank: Fusilier
DoB: 18.11.1922

WHITEHOUSE Frank
Service: Army - 14727500
Regt: K.O.S.B., H.L.I., 53rd Welsh Div.
Rank: Pte.
DoB: 4.9.1925

WHITEMAN David
Service: Army - 7363389
Regt: 181 Air Landing, Field Amb. 1st A.B. Div.
Rank: Pte.
DoB: 7.8.1919

WHITWELL Ray
Service: Army - 122205
Regt: 250 Light Comp Coy. R.A.S.C. 1st A.B. Div.
Rank: Driver
DoB: 17.3.1919

WILDERSPIN Reg
Service: Army - W/14732472
Regt: R.A.S.C., 21st Army Group
Rank: W/Cpl.
DoB: 30.3.1925

WOJCIECHOWSKI Josef
Service: Army - 25317
Regt: 1st Polish Indep. Para. Bde.
Rank: L/Cpl.
DoB: 28.9.1922

The Touring Party

Papendal Hotel, Oosterbeek

Saturday 2nd May 2015

Parkeston Quay Railway Club

The Taxis with veterans, carers and supporters rendezvoused at the Railway Club prior to embarking the Stena Ferry for the overnight sailing to Hook van Holland. The club provided refreshments and entertainment.

Harry Bailey R.A.S.C. Pioneer Corps Coy. and Driver Julian Lillington

Don Turrell (Left)

Cameronians, Scottish Rifles
46th (Highland) Infantry Bde.
15th Scottish Infantry Division

Ernie Marshall (Right)
52nd Beds Yeomanry Heavy Regiment R.A.

The Colchester Band

Drivers **Graham Pike** (left) and **Fred Jones** (holding beers)

Harold Herbert 10th Bn. Parachute Regiment, 1st Airborne Division

The Ferry

Boarding the Stena Ferry at the port of Harwich

Alan Reid Royal Navy, H.M.S. Balsam K72 Flower Class Corvette

Sunday 3rd May 2015

Disembarking the Stena Ferry at the Hook van Holland

Walter Price

R.A.F., 294 Sqn., Air Sea Rescue

Charles Jeffries

Highland Light Infantry, 53rd Welsh Division

Piper Chic Mackie

1st Bn. Black Watch

Bert Everson

Royal Tank Regiment

Alex Lambeth

Merchant Navy, Troop Ships,
Att. O.H.M.S.

Willam Stannard

1st Bn. Royal Fusiliers

Joe Sealey

Royal Signals

129th Infantry Brigade Signals

43rd Wessex Division

Konstanty Staszkiewicz
3rd Bn. Paratroop Brigade
1st Polish Independent

Harry Grew
Royal Navy, H.M.S. Starwort, Westcott,
Highway and Dido

John Sleep
Parachute Regiment
Att. 1st Bn. Norfolk Regiment

Bronbeek Veterans' Home, Arnhem

A warm Dutch welcome on the road to the Bronbeek Veterans' Home

Don Turrell Cameronians (Scottish Rifles) 46th Highland Infantry Brigade, 15th Scottish Infantry Division

Driver **David Webb** (holding umbrella)

Luis DiMarco 1st Bn. Parachute Regiment, 1st Airborne Division

With Carer Matthew Lucas

Len Brace Royal Signals, II Air Formation Signals Regiment

John (Jack) Kendall 179th Field Regiment, Royal Artillery

Presentations and Speeches

Jeffrey Haward M.M.

1/7th Bn. Middlesex Regiment

51st Highland Division

Receiving the lapel pin of the
Dutch White Carnation,
Flower of Liberation.

Ted Pieri

250 Comp 1st Airborne Division

63 Comp 6th Airborne Division

Ian Pieri attaches Ted's lapel pin of the
Dutch White Carnation, Flower of Liberation.

Lt. General Ted Meines

Presentation of 'Return of The Liberators 1945-2015' Crystal Plates

Henry Kubinski

65 Coy. R.A.S.C., 18 Amphib Coy.

612 Tank Transport Coy. R.A.S.C. RCT

16 Tank Trans Sqn. RCT

Walter Hart

Royal Army Medical Corps

George Empson

R.E.M.E. Att. 2/7th Bn. Middlesex Regiment

Douglas Tooke

6th Airborne Division, RECCE Sqn.

Charles Bailey

R.A.S.C., 58 BSD

Henry Harper

R.A.S.C. 1st & 6th Airborne Divisions

Hartenstein Museum, Oosterbeek

On the road to the Hartenstein Museum, Oosterbeek

Roland Dane 7th Bn. Black Watch, 51st Highland Division

Patrick Ready
Royal Marine Commando, N458 Flotilla LCP

Charlie Francis R.A.S.C., 743 Comp
Ken Watts 2nd Bn. Devonshire Regiment (Behind in Taxi)

Michael Brown 'E' Sqn. Glider Pilot Regiment

Luis DiMarco

1st Bn. Parachute Regiment

1st Airborne Division

Hartenstein Museum, Oosterbeek

Ron Johnson

'E' Sqn. Glider Pilot Regiment

Hartenstein Museum, Oosterbeek

Bob Stevens

Royal Engineers

Alf Lonsdale

Royal Navy, H.M.S. Valiant, Malaya, Tyne, Berwick and Glengyle

Percy Moss

Royal Suffolk Hussars

55th Anti-Tank Regiment

Frank Pendergast

7th (LI) Bn. Parachute Regiment

6th Airborne Division

Frank Whitehouse

King's Own Scottish Borderers

53rd Welsh Division

Arnie Hutchinson

7th (LI) Bn. Parachute Regiment

6th Airborne Division

David Whiteman 181 Air Landing, Field Ambulance, 1st Airborne Division

Ray Whitwell 250 Light Comp Coy. R.A.S.C., 1st Airborne Division

Evening entertainment at the Papendal Hotel, Oosterbeek

Top, holding flags, left to right: **Dennis James**, **Eddie Hillery** and 'Barking Bill' (**Terry Ward**)

Dickie Forrester 2nd Bn. King's Royal Rifle Corps, 4th Armoured Brigade, dancing with **Gill Ward**

Monday 4th May 2015

The Groesbeek Canadian War Cemetery and Memorial

Wreath laying and service at Groesbeek.

The Rev'd. George Parsons No 2 Army Commando, Royal Fusiliers, conducting the service, committee members to his right

The standard of The London Taxi Benevolent
Association For War Disabled

Les Eastwood
Royal Navy, H.M.S. Copra, Landing Craft

Left: Tom Schaffer Parachute Regiment
Right: Paul Davis Committee Member

The Last Post

Roland Dane 7th Bn. Black Watch, 51st Highland Division

John Charles Penrose Coode 1st Bn. King's Own Scottish Borderers and his wife Nicola

Ted Pieri

250 Comp 1st Airborne Division

63 Comp 6th Airborne Division

John Riley

Anti-Tank Regiment, Royal Artillery

Albert Gardner

Royal Engineers and

Royal West African Frontier Force

Roy Cadman

The Buffs, No 3 Army Commando

Alfred John Court

3rd Royal Tank Regiment

15th Armoured Brigade

Abba Myer Malin

185th Field Regiment, R.A. 49th Division

186th Field Regiment, R.A. 52nd Division

The National Liberation Museum Groesbeek

Entertainment, lunch and meeting the students

Michael Brown 'E' Sqn. Glider Pilot Regiment, handing out his cards

Dutch Remembrance Service, Town Hall, Arnhem

Geoff Pattinson 9th Bn. Parachute Regiment, 6th Airborne Division   Fred Glover 9th Bn. Parachute Regiment, 6th Airborne Division

Harold Herbert 10th Bn. Parachute Regiment, 1st Airborne Division   Joe McAllister 3rd Bn. Parachute Regiment, 1st Airborne Division

Michael Brown

'E' Sqn. Glider Pilot Regiment

Ken Washer

1st Airborne Division, RECCE Sqn.

Ron Johnson

'E' Sqn. Glider Pilot Regiment

Fred Walker

Beds and Herts Regiment

No 3 Army Commando

Frank Ashleigh

'A' Sqn. Glider Pilot Regiment

Edwin Brown

1st Bn. Parachute Regiment

Tuesday 5th May 2015

Service at the Oosterbeek Airborne Memorial, Hartenstein

Iain Bonner 'D' Sqn. Glider Pilot Regiment

John and Liz Stubbs
Medical Support Team

Konstanty Staszkiewicz
3rd Bn. Paratroop Bde., 1st Polish Independent

Ken Washer and wife Elena
1st Airborne Division, RECCE Sqn.

Geoffrey Roberts

7th Bn. King's Own Scottish Borderers

Airlanding Brigade

1st Airborne Division

George Barton

7th Bn. King's Own Scottish Borderers

Airlanding Brigade

1st Airborne Division

John Crosson

7th Bn. King's Own Scottish Borderers

Airlanding Brigade

1st Airborne Division

Josef Wojciechowski

1st Polish Independent Parachute Brigade

Des Page

'E' Sqn. Glider Pilot Regiment

The National Liberation Parade, Wageningen

Drivers prepared for the Liberation Parade

Clockwise from top left: **Peter Waterfield**, **Ian Gray**, **Dennis James** and **Chris Hearndon**

Driver **Steve Dolby**

The storm - National Liberation Parade, Wageningen

Before the parade could take place the heavens opened with prolonged heavy rain

Harry Grew
Royal Navy, H.M.S. Starwort, Westcott,
Highway and Dido

Ken West
11th Bn. Royal Scots Fusiliers

Right:

Des Page
'E' Sqn. Glider Pilot Regiment
assisted by **Dennis Hayes**
Driver and Committee Member

Don Hacker
Ox and Bucks Light Infantry
6th Airborne Division

Lawrence Martin

1st Division Airborne, Divisional Signals

James Corrigan

Durham Light Infantry

Don Hacker

Oxfordshire and Buckinghamshire Light Infantry

6th Airborne Division

John Jeffries

Royal Corps of Signals

4th Parachute Brigade 'K' Section

1st Airborne Division

Laurie Weeden

'F' Sqn. Glider Pilot Regiment

Ernest Davies

Royal Navy, H.M.S. Cotton

The Final Night

Papendal Hotel, speeches and presentations

Members of the Charity Committee The London Taxi Benevolent Association For War Disabled

Chairman Gary Belsey presents a bouquet to Susy Goodwin

Driver Danny Bedford (left) filming Danny McCrudden Royal Navy, H.M.S. Queensborough and Implacable

Percy Lewis

1st Bucks Bn.

1st Bn. Black Watch

Reginald (Stan) Daines

2nd Bn. Essex Regiment

4th Bn. Dorset Regiment

George Lines

Royal Signals, H.Q. 4th Army, Royal Artillery

Danny McCrudden

Royal Navy

H.M.S. Queensborough & Implacable

Bill Gladden

6th Airborne Division, Armoured RECCE

Ken West

11th Bn. Royal Scots Fusiliers

Wednesday 6th May 2015

The final day

Collectors (left to right): Bill Parr, Charles Jeffries, Dickie Forrester and George Stagg 168th Coy., Royal Engineers

Dick Goodwin presented a 'Return of The Liberators 1945-2015' Crystal Plate to Anouk Keutentjes, Events Organiser for the Papendal Hotel

The Journey Home

Piper Chic Mackie 1st Bn. Black Watch - Leads the departure from the Papendal Hotel

On The Ferry

Service and laying of wreaths for 'Those Lost at Sea'

Top Left to right: **The Rev'd George Parsons**, Colin Wright, Fred Harris and Tom Schaffer

Bottom: **Alan Reid** Royal Navy, H.M.S. Balsam K72 Flower Class Corvette

Father Ted Rogers
Merchant Navy

The Rev'd. George Parsons
No 2 Army Commando, Royal Fusiliers

Jeffrey Haward M.M. 1/7th Bn. Middlesex Regiment, 51st Highland Division

Alan Reid
Royal Navy
H.M.S. Balsam K72 Flower Class Corvette

Peter Kent

Royal Navy

H.M.S. Adventure and Hartland Point

Fred Harris

Royal Engineers, 621st Field Sqn.

7th Armoured Division

John Grange

Comm. of Signals, Royal Signals

16th Independent Parachute Brigade

Henry (Buzz) Brown

Combined Opps., 330 Support Sqn.

Harry Rice

4th Bn. Norfolks Royal Artillery

1st Bn. Parachute Regiment

1st Airborne Division

Jim Knox

Royal East Kent Regiment

4th Bn. Parachute Regiment

Alan Hartley

RAF, 271 Sqn., Transport Command

Bill Martin

7th Bn. (L.I.) Parachute Regiment, 6th Airborne Division

Iain Bonner 'D' Sqn. Glider Pilot Regiment

A tiring day

Veterans resting on the journey home

William Spring 323 Bty. 81st Field Regiment, R.A., 53rd Welsh Division

Harry Grew Royal Navy H.M.S. Starwort, Westcott, Highway, Dido

Filming the trip

The film crew, directed by Janet Hodgson, documenting the trip

The film crew interviewing veteran **Des Page** 'E' Glider Pilot Regiment, near the Hartenstein Airborne Memorial, Oosterbeek

Filming on board the Stena Ferry

Roll of Honour

Veterans who have passed on since the trip:

William (Bill) Cantwell - 24th Field Regiment, R.A.

Fred Barefield - 11th Parachute Sqn. Royal Engineers

Henry (Buzz) Brown - Comb Opps. 330 Support Sqn.

Geoffrey Cottle - R.E.M.E.

Reginald (Stan) Daines - 2nd Bn. Essex Regiment, 4th Bn. Dorset Regiment

George French - King's Royal Rifle Corps

Harold Herbert - 10th Bn. Parachute Regiment, 1st Airborne Division

George Lines - Royal Signals, H.Q. 4th Army Group R.A.

Bill Martin - 7th Bn. (L.I.) Parachute Regiment, 6th Airborne Division

Ernie Morgan - R.A.S.C.

Patrick Ready - Royal Marine Commando N458 Flotilla LCP

Harry Rice - 4th Norfolks R.A., 1st Bn. Parachute Regiment, 1st Airborne Division

William Stannard - 1st Bn. Royal Fusiliers

Fred Walker - Beds & Herts, No 3 Army Commando

Keith Collman

Photographer and Designer

It was a privilege to be commissioned to create this photographic record, possibly the last pilgrimage of Second World War veterans on this scale.

In 1984 I went on a similar pilgrimage to the Old Western Front with veterans of the First World War, at the time they were of the same age. That was also to be the last of its kind.

The photographs I took in 1984 stimulated my desire to of meet more of these men and women; at reunions, on battlefield tours and visits to their homes.

In 2009 I published *'Great War Portraits'*, a photographic book featuring portraits of the First World War veterans I'd met over twenty five years.

I'm thankful the Charity decided to sponsor the production of this book in recognition of the veterans' service during World War Two.

Keith Collman

Previous publications

Great War Portraits
ISBN: 978-0-9563667-0-2
www.greatwarportraits.com

Photographic Equipment:
Olympus OM-D Digital Camera, Lumix 2.5/14mm & Olympus 12-50mm Zoom

Printing Data:
Cover: BVS Silk 150gsm, matt laminated
Text pages: BVS Silk 170gsm
Photographs: Duotone, Black and Pantone 404
Font: Optima